D0807342

African Interior Design

teNeues

Editor in chief: Paco Asensio

Project coordination: Alejandro Bahamón

Texts: Irantzu Piquero, Alejandro Bahamón

Editorial coordination: Haike Falkenberg

Research: Katharina Esser

Art director: Mireia Casanovas Soley

Layout: Soti Mas-Bagà

German translation: Susanne Engler

French translation: Lingo Sense S.L.

English translation: Wendy Griswold

© Photos p. 13–17: Miquel Tres

Published by teNeues Publishing Group

teNeues Publishing Company
16 West 22nd Street, New York, NY 10010, USA
Tel.: 001-212-627-9090, Fax: 001-212-627-9511

teNeues Book Division
Kaistraße 18
40221 Düsseldorf, Germany
Tel.: 0049-(0)211-994597-0, Fax: 0049-(0)211-994597-40

teNeues Publishing UK Ltd.
P.O. Box 402
West Byfleet
KT14 7ZF, Great Britain
Tel.: 0044-1932-403509, Fax: 0044-1932-403514

www.teneues.com

ISBN: 3-8238-4563-2

Editorial project: © 2003 LOFT Publications
Via Laietana 32, 4º Of. 92
08003 Barcelona, Spain
Tel.: 0034 932 688 088
Fax: 0034 932 687 073

e-mail: loft@loftpublications.com
www.loftpublications.com

Printed by: Anman Gràfiques del Vallès, Spain. 2004

Bibliographic information published by
Die Deutsche Bibliothek. Die Deutsche
Bibliothek lists this publication in the
Deutsche Nationalbibliografie;
detailed bibliographic data is available
in the Internet at http://dnb.ddb.de

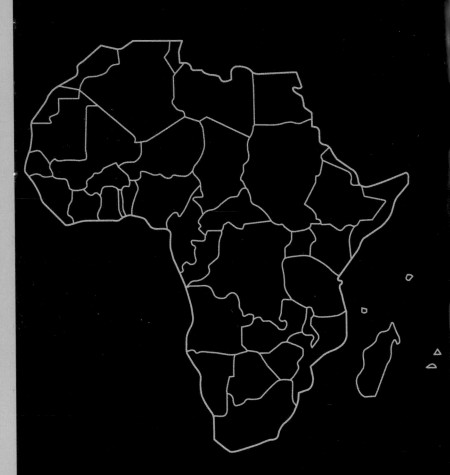

INTRODUCTION

The African continent is a melting pot, reflected in a variety of societal and cultural expressions. In this vast expanse we can find examples of the most primitive traditions and the most contemporary art and architecture. While the vast Sahara desert is a natural divide between northern Africa and the rest of the continent, there is much evidence of exchange between the two zones, thanks to trade routes that crossed the continent from the earliest times. Moreover, the various colonizations, principally by European countries, left a strong imprint on the local cultures. This book takes a fascinating tour of the continent's recent domestic architecture, encompassing more than 43 projects that masterfully handle every detail of structural and interior design. While each project responds specifically to the nature of its setting, there are also common threads, such as references to tribal cultures, natural materials, and earth colors. Each project clearly reflects the times and the cultural influences on the area, and in each, the architects and designers create a unique and undeniably African style.

EINLEITUNG

Auf dem afrikanischen Kontinent treffen zahlreiche Kulturen aufeinander, die sich in einer Vielzahl von sozialen und kulturellen Ausdrucksweisen widerspiegeln. Auf diesem großen Territorium sind deshalb sowohl Beispiele für die primitivsten Traditionen des Menschen als auch für moderne, zeitgenössische Kunst und Architektur zu finden. Obwohl die große Wüste Sahara eine natürliche Grenze zwischen Nordafrika und dem restlichen Kontinent bildet, gibt es viele Beweise für den Einfluss beider Zonen aufeinander, bedingt durch die Handelsrouten, die schon seit frühester Zeit den Kontinent durchkreuzen. Außerdem haben die verschiedenen Kolonisierungen durch die europäischen Länder tiefe Spuren im kulturellen Ausdruck hinterlassen. Dieses Buch schlägt eine interessante Reise durch die moderne Wohnhausarchitektur des Kontinents vor. Es werden 43 verschiedene Häuser vorgestellt, in denen mit großer Meisterschaft alle Einzelheiten der Architektur und Innenarchitektur gestaltet wurden. Obwohl jedes dieser Häuser dem Charakter seiner Umgebung entspricht, sind doch auch bei allen gemeinsame Elemente zu finden, so z. B. Entlehnungen aus den Stammeskulturen und die Verwendung natürlicher Materialien und Erdfarben. An jedem Haus sind deutlich die Epochen und Kulturen zu erkennen, die in der jeweiligen Region eine Rolle spielen oder spielten. Dennoch wurde durch die Arbeit der Architekten und Innenarchitekten ein eigener Stil erreicht, der gleichzeitig unverwechselbar afrikanisch ist.

Le continent africain réunit de nombreuses cultures, reflétées par une réelle diversité d'expressions sociales et culturelles. Ce vaste territoire s'offre aux rencontres d'exemples des traditions les plus primitives jusqu'aux plus contemporaines de l'hommes à travers l'art et l'architecture. Bien que le vaste désert du Sahara se pose en barrière séparant naturellement le Nord de l'Afrique du reste du continent, de nombreuses preuves confirment toute une série d'influences entre ces deux zones grâce aux routes commerciales traversant le continent depuis des temps immémoriaux. De même, les diverses colonisations, essentiellement l'œuvre de pays européens, ont laissé des traces importantes dans les expressions culturelles. Cet ouvrage propose un parcours intéressant de l'architecture domestique la plus récente du continent à travers le prisme de plus de 43 projets de demeures résolvant magistralement chaque détail architectural et de design d'intérieur. Bien que chaque projet corresponde de façon spécifique aux caractéristiques de son environnement, ils permettent tous de relever des traits communs, ainsi les références aux cultures tribales, aux matériaux naturels et aux couleurs terre. Chacun nous offre une visualisation claire des époques et cultures affectant la zone en question où, sous la houlette d'architectes et de designer, naît un style personnel et, incontestablement, africain.

En el continente africano se reúne una gran cantidad de culturas, reflejadas en una variedad de expresiones sociales y culturales. En esta vasta extensión de territorio podemos encontrar desde muestras de las más primitivas tradiciones del hombre hasta los ejemplos más contemporáneos de arte y arquitectura. Aunque la gran extensión del desierto del Sahara actúa como barrera divisoria natural entre el norte de África y el resto del continente, hay muchas evidencias que confirman toda una serie de influencias entre ambas zonas a través de rutas comerciales que atravesaron el continente desde tiempos remotos. Asimismo las diversas colonizaciones, principalmente por países europeos, han dejado huellas importantes en las expresiones culturales. En este libro se propone un interesante recorrido a través de la arquitectura doméstica más reciente del continente a través de más de 43 proyectos de vivienda que resuelven con maestría cada detalle de arquitectura y diseño interior. Aunque cada proyecto responde de modo específico a las características de su entorno, en todos se pueden destacar algunos rasgos comunes como las referencias a las culturas tribales, los materiales naturales o los colores tierra. En cada uno de ellos podemos visualizar claramente las épocas y culturas que afectan a esta zona y en donde, de la mano de arquitectos y diseñadores, se logra un estilo propio e inconfundiblemente africano.

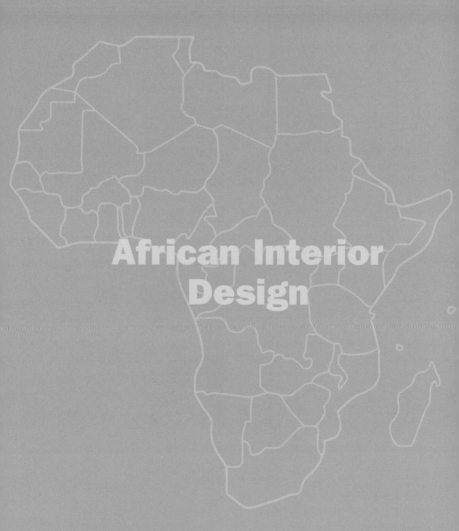

African Interior Design

Noor el Gurna

Architect: **By the owner**
Location: **Luxor, Egypt**
Photos: © **Ricardo Labougle, Hugo Curletto**

A natural fiber roof, beds of bamboo with mosquito netting, and hand-crafted rugs are the austere components of these rooms, in which time seems to have stood still. Located between the Valley of the Kings and the Valley of the Queens, this building, as is typical of older structures in northern Egypt, is made of adobe.

Die Decke aus Naturfasern, die Bambusbetten mit Moskitonetz und die handgearbeiteten Teppiche sind die einfachen Elemente, die diese Räume beherrschen. Die Zeit scheint hier stillzustehen. Das zwischen dem Tal der Könige und Tal der Königinnen gelegene Haus aus Luftziegeln ist ein typisches Gebäude aus dem Norden des Landes.

Le toit de fibre naturelle, les lits de bambou à moustiquaire et les tapis artisanaux sont les éléments austères composant cette demeure où le temps semble s'être arrêté. Entre la vallée des Rois et des Reines, le bâtiment présente des murs en pisé, typiques des anciennes constructions du nord du pays.

El techo de fibra natural, las camas de bambú con mosquitera y las alfombras artesanales del lugar son los austeros elementos que componen estas estancias en las que parece haberse detenido el tiempo. Entre el valle de los Reyes y de las Reinas, el edificio está hecho con adobe, típico en construcciones antiguas del norte del país.

Salome's Garden

Architects: **Tom Green, Nigel V. Brown**
Location: **Zanzibar, Tanzania**
Photos: © **Manolo Yllera**

This small, ancient palace dates back to the early nineteenth century and once belonged to Princess Salome. It takes its inspiration from Islamic architecture and ornamentation. Behind its thick and now somewhat decayed walls is a home with a tropical garden that stretches to the sea. The carved doors are a fine example of Zanzibari craftsmanship.

Dieser alte Palast vom Beginn des 19. Jh. gehörte der Prinzessin Salome. Architektur und Dekorationen sind islamisch inspiriert. Hinter den dicken, leicht verfallenen Mauern verbirgt sich ein Haus, dessen tropischer Garten sich bis zum Meer erstreckt. Die geschnitzten Türen sind typische Beispiele des Handwerks in Sansibar.

Cet ancien palais début XIXème appartenait à la princesse Salomé ; d'architecture et d'ornementation d'inspiration islamique, il abrite derrière ses murs épais, et quelque peu en ruines, une demeure servant d'antichambre à un jardin tropical rejoignant la mer. Ses portes taillées sont un exemple d'artisanat de Zanzibar.

Este antiguo palacete de comienzos del XIX perteneció a la princesa Salomé; con su arquitectura y ornamentación de inspiración islámica, contiene tras sus gruesos y ya algo arruinados muros una vivienda que sirve de antesala a un jardín tropical que llega hasta el mar. Sus puertas talladas son una muestra de la artesanía zanzibarí.

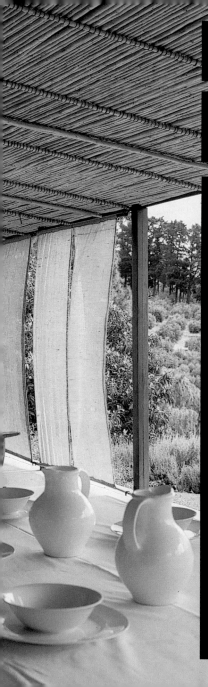

Weekend

Architect: **By the owner**

Location: **Cape Town, South Africa**

Photos: © **Redcover / Ken Hayden**

This weekend home is striking for the simple way it combines rustic elements, either integral to the architecture or as part of the decor, with contemporary objects to create a functional and modern space. Wood is prominent in the totally renovated kitchen and bathroom.

Dieses Wochenendhaus zeichnet sich durch die Nüchternheit aus, mit der die rustikalen Elemente der Architektur und die Formen der Dekorationselemente mit zeitgenössischen Objekten kombiniert sind, so dass ein funktionelles und modernes Gebäude entsteht. Das wichtigste Material in der renovierten Küche und dem Bad ist das Holz.

Cette résidence de week-end se distingue par la sobriété voyant la conjugaison des éléments rustiques, intégrés à l'architecture ou en pièces décoratives, et des objets contemporains pour créer un espace fonctionnel et moderne. Cuisine et bains, entièrement rénovés, mêlent essentiellement le bois comme matériau principal.

Esta residencia de fin de semana destaca por la sobriedad con la que se conjugan elementos rústicos, incorporados a la arquitectura o en forma de piezas decorativas, junto a objetos contemporáneos que crean un espacio funcional y moderno. La cocina y el baño, completamente renovados, mezclan siempre la madera como materia prima.

Classic and White

Architect: : By the owner
Location: Cape Town, South Africa
Photos: © Redcover / Wayne Vincent

Natural light filtering through the wooden blinds creates a fresh, warm effect in the interior of this house. The décor takes the South African colonial era as a reference point, emphasizing classical elements such as the upholstery, heavy fabrics, and floral motifs.

Das Tageslicht, das durch die Holzjalousien fällt, schafft eine frische und warme Atmosphäre in diesem Haus, das klassische Elemente der kolonialen Architektur Südafrikas bewahrt. Die Dekoration ist durch jene Epoche inspiriert, und es tauchen Elemente wie Polster, schwere Stoffe und Blumenmotive auf.

La lumière naturelle, filtrant des persiennes en bois, crée un effet frais et chaleureux dans cette maison, préservant les éléments classiques de l'architecture coloniale sud-africaine. La décoration prend cette époque pour référence et récupère des principes tels le capitonnage, les toiles pesantes et les motifs floraux.

La luz natural que se filtra a través de las persianas de madera crea un efecto fresco y cálido en el interior de esta casa que guarda elementos clásicos de la arquitectura colonial sudafricana. La decoración toma como referencia esta época y recupera elementos como el capitoneado, telas pesadas y motivos floridos.

Artist's House

Architect: **By the owner**
Location: **Essaouira, Morocco**
Photos: © **Reto Guntli / Zapaimages**

The originality of the architecture and the exceptional location of this house, right on the seacoast of Essaouira, southern Morocco, were the basis for the interior design theme. Original elements, such as the glazed ceramic tiles and the woodwork, were preserved.

Die originelle Bauweise und die einzigartige Lage direkt am Meer in Essaouira im Süden Marokkos sind die entscheidenden Faktoren für die Innengestaltung dieses Wohnhauses. Die ursprünglichen Elemente des Baus wie Kacheln und Holzarbeiten wurden erhalten.

Le caractère original de la demeure et sa situation privilégiée, face à la mer à Essaouira, au sud du Maroc, sont les facteurs déterminants du design intérieur de la résidence. Les éléments d'origine de la construction ont été préservés, ainsi les céramiques et la charpente.

El carácter original de la construcción así como la situación privilegiada de esta casa, totalmente enfrentada al mar en Essaouira, al sur de Marruecos, son los factores determinantes para el diseño interior de la residencia. Se han conservado los elementos originales de la construcción como los azulejos y la carpintería.

Moroccan Palace

Architect: **Charles Boccara**
Location: **Duar Abiat, Morocco**
Photos: © **Pere Planells**

This early twentieth century palace in southern Morocco has been restored with great mastery, respecting the precious decorative elements. It is organized around two courtyards, one paved with stone and the other filled with dense plant life. The interior is noteworthy for its fine exposed brickwork.

Dieser zu Beginn des vergangenen Jahrhunderts im Süden Marokkos errichtete Palast wurde meisterhaft restauriert und die wertvollen Dekorationselemente weitgehend erhalten. Die Räume verteilen sich um einen steinernen und einen bepflanzten Innenhof. Im Inneren fallen die eleganten Arbeiten aus unverputztem Ziegelstein auf.

Au sud du Maroc, ce palais début XXème a été restauré avec maîtrise, en respectant au maximum les éléments décoratifs précieux formant son architecture. La maison s'organise autour de deux patios, l'un en pierre et l'autre à la végétation dense. À l'intérieur se distingue la finesse du travail de la brique apparente.

Este palacio de principios de siglo al sur de Marruecos ha sido rehabilitado con gran maestría respetando al máximo los valiosos elementos decorativos que conforman su arquitectura. La casa se organiza en torno a dos patios, uno pétreo y otro con una densa vegetación. En el interior destaca el fino trabajo de ladrillo a la vista.

Simplicity

Architect: **Lionel Edwards**
Location: **Cape Town, South Africa**
Photos: **© Redcover / Craig Fraser**

This home is a long structure with an exposed wooden framework, an ideal venue for a project halfway between rustic and contemporary. A range of earth tones, from brown to white, creates a warm, comfortable atmosphere inside.

Dieses Wohnhaus ist in einer länglichen Hütte mit sichtbarer Holzstruktur untergebracht, die einen idealen Rahmen für eine halb rustikale, halb zeitgenössische Gestaltung bildet. Die Innendekoration wurde in verschiedenen Erdtönen – von braun bis weiß – gehalten, wodurch die Räume warm und einladend wirken.

Cette demeure habite un chalet longitudinal à structure de bois apparente, s'offrant en cadre idéal pour créer un projet à mi-chemin du rustique et du contemporain. Le design intérieur a vu le choix d'une palette de tons terreux, du marron au blanc, générant une atmosphère chaleureuse et confortable.

Esta vivienda se ubica en una cabaña longitudinal de estructura de madera a la vista, sirviendo de marco ideal para crear un proyecto a medio camino entre lo rústico y lo contemporáneo. Para el diseño interior se ha elegido una gama de tonos tierra, que van del marrón al blanco, logrando un ambiente cálido y confortable.

Architect: **Anton de Kock**

Location: **Cape Town, South Africa**

Photos: © **Redcover / Craig Fraser**

The design of this apartment, which enjoys marvelous views of the city, is based on a mix of colors and styles that achieves a decidedly contemporary effect. The different rooms are connected and subtly demarcated by using contrasting colors on certain walls or changes in the type and texture of the flooring.

Die Gestaltung dieser Wohnung mit wundervollem Blick auf die Stadt basiert auf dem Vermischen von Farben und Stilen, was sie absolut zeitgenössisch wirken lässt. Die Räume werden durch einzelne, farbige Mauern oder Bodenbeläge aus wechselnden Materialien oder Texturen miteinander verbunden und subtil voneinander abgegrenzt.

Le design de cet appartement, offrant de superbes panoramas sur la ville, repose sur un mélange de couleurs et de styles créant une ambiance définitivement contemporaine. Les diverses pièces sont reliées et subtilement délimitées par des murs libres de couleur ou des changements de type ou de texture du sol.

El diseño de este apartamento, que cuenta con amplias panorámicas de la ciudad, se basa en una mezcla de colores y estilos logrando un ambiente decididamente contemporáneo. Las diferentes estancias están relacionadas y sutilmente demarcadas por muros sueltos de color o cambios en el tipo y textura del pavimento.

Chapwani Island

Architects: **Maura Antonietto, Nigel V. Brown**
Location: **Chapwani Island, Zanzibar, Tanzania**
Photos: © **Manolo Yllera**

The island, on an ancient route used by traders, adventurers, and explorers, is the idyllic backdrop for this structure, which resembles the traditional homes found in the archipelago. The vaulting, the rustic charm of the furnishings, fabrics with African motifs, and beds with mosquito netting are details that make it unique.

Die Insel, auf der einstigen Route der Händler, Abenteurer und Entdeckungsreisenden gelegen, ist die idyllische Umgebung dieses Gebäudes, das die traditionelle Bauweise der Inseln imitiert. Die Gewölbe, bezaubernd einfache Möbel, Stoffe mit afrikanischen Motiven und Betten mit Moskitonetz als Baldachin machen es einzigartig.

L'île, sur l'ancienne route des marchands, aventuriers et explorateurs, offre un cadre idyllique à la construction affectant le style des demeures traditionnelles de l'archipel. Les voûtes, la rudesse du charme du mobilier, les toiles aux motifs africains et les lits à moustiquaire sont les détails qui la rendent unique.

La isla, situada en una antigua ruta de mercaderes, aventureros y exploradores, es el escenario idílico para esta construcción que emula las viviendas tradicionales del archipiélago. Las bóvedas, el rudo encanto de los muebles, las telas con motivos africanos y camas con dosel de mosquitera son los detalles que lo hacen único.

Tribal Art

Architect: **By the owner**
Location: **Cape Town, South Africa**
Photos: © **Redcover / Colin Sharp**

Utilitarian and decorative artifacts produced by African tribal cultures are the principal interior design elements of this house. The collections, consisting mainly of wooden objects, create a unique atmosphere in each room, and great richness of texture in every nook and cranny.

Die Gebrauchsgegenstände und dekorativen Objekte der afrikanischen Stämme sind die grundlegenden Elemente der Innenausstattung dieses Hauses. Die verschiedenen Objektsammlungen, hauptsächlich aus Holz, schaffen in allen Räumen eine einzigartige Atmosphäre, so dass jeder Winkel reich verziert ist.

Les artefacts utilitaires et décoratifs, produits de cultures tribales africaines, sont les éléments clés du design intérieur de cette maison. Chaque collection d'objet, principalement en bois, crée une atmosphère unique déterminée pour chaque pièce, afin que chaque recoin bénéficie d'une grande richesse de textures.

Los artefactos utilitarios y decorativos producidos por culturas tribales africanas son los elementos principales en el diseño interior de esta casa. Cada colección de objetos, principalmente de madera, crea una atmósfera determinada para cada una de las estancias logrando que en cada rincón haya una gran riqueza de texturas.

Tigmi Tagadert

Architect: **Max Lawrence**
Location: **Tagadert, Morocco**
Photos: © **Pere Planells**

The original elements of rural Moroccan architecture, such as adobe walls, roofs made of reeds, and floors of natural stone, have been restored to create a luxury home in the countryside. Colored rugs, cushions, and draperies combine to create a warm, refreshing atmosphere.

Um ein luxuriöses Wohnhaus auf dem Lande zu schaffen, wurden die typischen Elemente der ländlichen, marokkanischen Architektur wie Mauern aus Luftziegeln, Rohrdächer und Böden aus Natursteinen verwendet. Bunte Teppiche, Kissen und Gardinen schaffen eine einladende und wohltuende Atmosphäre.

Les éléments originaux de l'architecture rurale marocaine – murs en pisé, toits en rotin ou sols en pierre naturelle – ont été récupérés pour créer une demeure luxueuse au cœur de la campagne. Tapis, coussins et rideaux de couleur engendrent une atmosphère chaleureuse et rafraîchissante.

Los elementos originales de la arquitectura campestre marroquí, como los muros de adobe, los techos de madera de caña o los suelos de piedra natural, se han recuperado para crear una vivienda de lujo en medio del campo. Por medio de alfombras, cojines y cortinas de colores se logra una atmósfera cálida y refrescante.

Ecological Dream

Architects: **Georg Fiebig, Jan Huelsemann,**
           Per Krushe
Location: **Chumbe Island, Tanzania**
Photos: © **Manolo Yllera**

This building's contemporary vaulting stands out against the tropical landscape of Chumbe, an island known for the coral reef that surrounds it. In a quest for true harmony with nature, everything was made of local materials, with mechanisms that ensure energy self-sufficiency.

Die modernen Gewölbe dieses Hauses auf Chumbe, einer Insel mit einem berühmten Korallenriff, heben sich gegen die tropische Landschaft ab. Alles ist aus örtlichen Materialien gefertigt, so dass ein wirkliches Zusammenspiel mit der Natur gefunden und ein autonomes Energie- und Recyclingsystem geschaffen wurde.

Les voûtes modernistes se détachent dans le paysage tropical, nous révélant cette construction de Chumbe, île célèbre pour la barrière de corail la ceignant. Tout est fabriqué à partir de matériaux locaux, en quête d'une coexistence réelle avec la nature et afin de créer un système énergétique et de recyclage autosuffisant.

Las bóvedas modernistas destacan sobre el paisaje tropical descubriéndonos esta construcción en Chumbe, isla conocida por la barrera de coral que la rodea. Todo está fabricado con materiales locales buscando una verdadera convivencia con la naturaleza y creando un sistema de utilización de energía y reciclado autosuficiente.

Riad Zina

Architect: **Beate Prinz**
Location: **Marrakesh, Morocco**
Photos: © **Manolo Yllera**

An oasis in the heart of the chaotic maze of Marrakech's zoco (large market), this riyad is an invitation to rest or gather. Doors with half-pointed horseshoe arches, windows with wrought iron grilles overlooking the interior courtyard, and the explosion of color in the mosaics on the walls, are typically Spanish-Moroccan decorative touches.

Dieser Riad ist eine Oase in dem chaotischen Labyrinth des Zoco (großer Markt) von Marrakesch, in dem man sich trifft und ausruht. Türen mit Hufeisen- und Rundbögen, Fenster mit schmiedeeisernen Gittern zum Innenhof und die farbenfrohen Mosaike der Wände sind typisch hispanisch-marokkanische Dekorationselemente.

Oasis au cœur du labyrinthe chaotique du souk de Marrakech, ce riad invite au repos et à la discussion. Portes aux arches outrepassées et semi-circulaires, fenêtres aux grilles forgées sur le patio intérieur, explosion de couleurs des mosaïques sur les murs : des éléments décoratifs typiquement hispano-marocains.

Oasis en el corazón del caótico laberinto del Zoco de Marrakech, este riad es una invitación al descanso y la tertulia. Puertas con arco de herradura y medio punto, ventanas con enrejado de forja hacia el patio interior y la explosión de color del mosaico en las paredes son elementos decorativos típicamente hispano-marroquíes.

A Fashion Designer's House

Architect: **Marianne Fassler**

Location: **Johannesburg, South Africa**

Photos: © **Deidi von Schaewen / Omnia**

The interior is an intense, warm explosion of color in which African decorative elements blend with western furnishings spanning different eras. The resulting combination, graced by the natural light pouring in through the windows, produces an eclectic, warm, and striking effect.

Das Innere gleicht einer intensiven und warmen Explosion von Farben, in der afrikanische Dekorationselemente mit ästhetischen Komponenten verschiedener Epochen der westlichen Welt zusammenfließen. Ergebnis ist eine eklektische, warme und auffällige Atmosphäre, gedämpft durch das Licht, das durch die Glasfenster dringt.

L'espace intérieur offre une explosion de couleurs chaudes et intenses faisant confluer les éléments décoratifs africains comme des composants esthétiques de diverses époques de la tradition occidentale. La combinaison résultante, nuancée par la lumière des baies vitrées, crée une atmosphère éclectique, chaude et attirante.

El espacio interior ofrece una intensa y cálida explosión de color en la que elementos decorativos africanos confluyen con componentes estéticos de distintas épocas de la tradición occidental. La combinación resultante, matizada por la luz procedente de las vidrieras, crea una atmósfera ecléctica, cálida y llamativa.

145

Elemental Evocation

Architect: **Torrisi**

Location: **Cape Town, South Africa**

Photos: **© Redcover / Colin Sharp**

This contemporary home is ideal for exhibiting a varied sampling of modern artwork and pieces of South African folk art. The white which dominates the interior is broken by touches of color and texture such as the wood panels and exposed stone.

Die Architektur dieses Wohnhauses, das als idealer Hintergrund für die Ausstellung moderner und südafrikanischer, volkstümlicher Kunstwerke dient, ist im zeitgenössischen Stil gehalten. Das Weiß, das sich über die Räume ergießt, wird durch etwas Farbe und Texturen wie Holzpaneele oder unverputzte Steine unterbrochen.

Un style contemporain personnalise l'architecture de cette demeure, site idéal d'exposition d'une multitude d'exemples d'art moderne et de pièces d'art folklorique sud-africain. Le blanc inondant l'espace intérieur est entrecoupé de touches de couleur et de texture, ainsi les panneaux de bois ou la pierre apparente.

Un estilo contemporáneo compone la arquitectura de esta vivienda, que sirve de escenario ideal para exhibir una variada muestra de arte moderno y piezas de arte folclórico sudafricano. El blanco que inunda el espacio interior se ve interrumpido por toques de color y textura como los paneles de madera o la piedra a la vista.

147

Atlantic Vacation

Architects: **Clinton McMurtie, Lee Messinger**
/ Creative Spaces
Location: **Cape Town, South Africa**
Photos: © **Redcover / Craig Fraser**

The blue of the Atlantic Ocean becomes the main compositional theme of this project, which is dominated by open, bright, clear spaces. The few pieces of contemporary furniture are carefully placed for best enjoyment of the splendid panoramic view of the sea and the suburbs of Cape Town.

Das Blau des Atlantischen Ozeans wird zum Entwurfsthema dieses Gebäudes, bei dem die offenen und hellen Räume dominieren. Die wenigen, zeitgenössischen Möbelstücke sind mit Sorgfalt angeordnet, so dass man den wundervollen Blick auf das Meer und die Vorstädte von Kapstadt genießen kann.

Le bleu de l'Atlantique devient le thème de la composition de ce projet où prédominent les espaces ouverts, lumineux et clairs. Les pièces de mobilier contemporain minimales sont disposées avec soin afin de profiter du splendide panorama sur la mer et les alentours de la Ville du Cap.

El azul del océano Atlántico se convierte en el tema compositivo de este proyecto en donde predominan los espacios abiertos, luminosos y claros. Las mínimas piezas de mobiliario contemporáneo están cuidadosamente dispuestas para disfrutar de la espléndida panorámica del mar y los suburbios de Ciudad del Cabo.

Ceramic Art

Architect: **Barbara Jackson**

Location: **Cape Town, South Africa**

Photos: **© Reto Guntli / Zapaimages**

This home belongs to an artist who works mainly with ceramics and uses her home as a workshop. The pieces she produces and the objects of contemporary western and African art enrich every corner of this house, with its basic lines and exposed materials.

Dieses Wohnhaus gehört einer Künstlerin, die hauptsächlich mit Keramik arbeitet und ihr Haus als Atelier nutzt. Die von ihr geschaffenen Werke, afrikanische und zeitgenössische westliche Kunstobjekte, bereichern jeden Winkel des in einfachen Linien gehaltenen Hauses mit vielen sichtbaren Konstruktionselementen.

Cette demeure appartient à une artiste travaillant principalement des pièces de céramique et lui tient lieu d'atelier de travail. Les pièces qu'elle produit tout comme les objets d'art occidental contemporain ou africain enrichissent chaque recoin de la maison aux lignes basiques et aux matériaux apparents.

Esta vivienda pertenece a una artista que principalmente trabaja con piezas de cerámica y utiliza su casa también como taller de trabajo. Tanto las piezas que ella misma produce como los objetos de arte occidental contemporáneo o africano enriquecen cada rincón de esta casa de líneas básicas y materiales a la vista.

Dinarobin

Architect: **Maurice Giraud**

Location: **Mauritius Island**

Photos: © **Manolo Yllera**

Mauritius Island is known for its cultural mix, the result of endless Indian, Arab, Central African, French, and English colonizations. The architecture respects the natural environment, while the interior design reflects the blending of cultures, incorporating elements from all of them.

Typisch für Mauritius ist die kulturelle Mischung, die durch die unaufhörlichen Kolonisierungen durch Inder, Araber, Zentralafrikaner, Franzosen und Engländer entstand. Die Architektur geht respektvoll mit der Natur um, während die Innengestaltung all diese Kulturen widerspiegelt.

L'Île Maurice se caractérise par son melting-pot culturel, fruit d'incessantes colonisations indiennes, arabes, centrafricaines, françaises et anglaises. L'architecture répond à une approche respectueuse du cadre naturel, le design intérieur reflétant le mélange culturel intégrant des éléments de chacune de ces cultures.

Isla Mauricio se caracteriza por su mezcla cultural, fruto de incesantes colonizaciones indias, árabes, centroafricanas, francesas e inglesas. La arquitectura responde a un planteamiento respetuoso por el entorno natural mientras que en el diseño interior se refleja la mezcla cultural incorporando elementos de todas estas culturas.

Lodge in the Desert

Architect: **Chris Browne**

Location: **Namibian Desert, Namibia**

Photos: © **CCAfrica**

Set in an almost-lunar landscape of endless horizons, this home is dominated by glass and stone. The exterior blends perfectly with the severity and austerity of the desert, while the interior, with its straight lines and light colors, is elegant and welcoming.

Dieses von Glas und Stein beherrschte Gebäude befindet sich in einer Landschaft, die fast einer Mondlandschaft gleicht. Äußerlich fügt es sich in seiner Strenge und Nüchternheit perfekt in die Landschaft ein, während im Inneren durch gerade Linien und helle Farben eine elegante und einladende Atmosphäre geschaffen wurde.

Dans un paysage quasi lunaire aux horizons infinis, le verre et la pierre dominent ce projet. L'aspect extérieur de la maison se fond parfaitement avec la sévérité du désert alors que les intérieurs, aux lignes droites et aux couleurs claires, offrent une ambiance élégante et accueillante.

Ubicado en un paisaje casi lunar de infinitos horizontes, el cristal y la piedra predominan en este proyecto. El aspecto exterior de la casa se integra a la perfección con la severidad y austeridad del desierto, mientras que los interiores, con sus lineas rectas y colores claros, ofrecen un ambiente elegante y acogedor.

Dar Amane

Architect: **Quentin Vilboux**
Location: **Marrakesh, Morocco**
Photos: © **Manolo Yllera**

In this fabulous late nineteenth century interior, east meets west through the harmonic combination of a rustic style and contemporary decorative touches. The brightness of the space and the murmur of the fountain in the rectangular courtyard make it a perfect place in which to retreat from the world and relax for a while.

In diesen wundervollen, Ende des 19. Jh. gestalteten Räumen fließen der Osten und der Westen durch die harmonische Kombination eines rustikalen Stils und zeitgenössischer Dekoration zusammen. Die hellen Räume und das Rauschen des Springbrunnens im rechteckigen Innenhof schaffen eine entspannende Atmosphäre.

Ces fabuleux intérieurs fin XIXème volent confluer Orient et Occident grâce au mariage harmonieux d'un style rustique et de tendances décoratives contemporaines. La luminosité de l'espace liée à la rumeur de la fontaine provenant du patio rectangulaire offrent une atmosphère apaisante et idéale pour l'évasion.

En este fabuloso interior de finales del XIX confluyen Oriente y Occidente a través de la armónica combinación de un estilo rústico y de tendencias decorativas contemporáneas. La luminosidad del espacio junto con el rumor de la fuente proveniente del patio rectangular ofrecen una atmósfera relajante e idónea para la evasión.

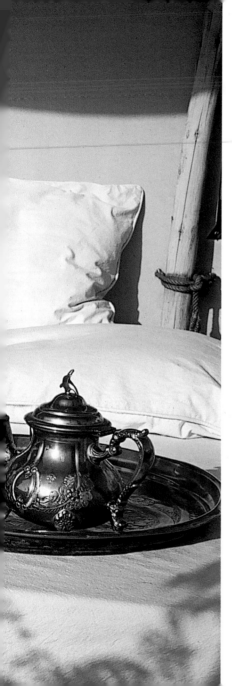

Golf Amelkis House

Architect: **Charles Boccara**
Location: **Marrakesh, Morocco**
Photos: © **Pere Planells**

This sumptuous house is an excellent example of the simplicity and elegance of Moroccan domestic architecture. Soft colors dominate each space, while fine details, such as the mosaics on the floors and coffered wood ceilings, enrich and add character to the interior.

Dieses prachtvolle Haus ist ein ausgezeichnetes Beispiel für die Schlichtheit und Eleganz, die so typisch für die marokkanische Architektur ist. Sanfte Farben beherrschen die Räume und erlesene Einzelheiten wie die Mosaiken der Böden oder die Deckentäfelung aus Holz verleihen ihnen ihren besonderen Charakter.

Cette somptueuse demeure est un excellent exemple de la sobriété et de l'élégance caractérisant l'architecture marocaine. Les tons pâles prédominent dans chaque espace alors que de légers détails – ainsi les mosaïques au sol ou les charpente au coffrage de bois – enrichissent et personnalisent l'espace intérieur.

Esta suntuosa casa es una excelente muestra de la sobriedad y elegancia que caracteriza la arquitectura doméstica marroquí. En cada espacio predomina el empleo de colores suaves mientras que finos detalles, como los mosaicos en los suelos o artesonados de madera en los techos, enriquecen y dan carácter al espacio interior.

Howard Green

Architect: **Richard Perfect**
Location: **Cape Town, South Africa**
Photos: © **Redcover / Wayne Vincent**

The original feel of this classic early twentieth century residence was retained to the greatest possible extent, by preserving period decorative elements and furnishings. Marble floors, dark wood parquet, plaster moldings, and some built-in components, notably in the kitchen, were restored.

Die ursprüngliche Atmosphäre in diesem klassischen Wohnhaus vom Anfang des 20. Jh. wurde so weit wie möglich respektiert, indem die Dekorationselemente und Möbel jener Epoche bewahrt wurden. Ebenso wurden die Marmorböden, das dunkle Holzparkett und das Gesims aus Gips und einige Einbaumöbel in der Küche erhalten.

L'atmosphère originale de cette résidence classique début XXème a été préservée au maximum en sauvant des éléments décoratifs et mobiliers de l'époque. Les sols en marbre comme le parquet en bois sombre mais aussi les moulures en plâtre et quelques meubles encastrés, ainsi celui de la cuisine, ont été sauvegardés.

La atmósfera original de esta residencia clásica de principios del siglo XX se ha mantenido al máximo rescatando elementos decorativos y mobiliario de la época. Se rescataron los suelos de mármol y el parqué de madera oscura así como las molduras de yeso y algunos muebles empotrados como el de la cocina.

Colonial Expansion

Architect: **By the owner**
Location: **Cape Town, South Africa**
Photos: © **Redcover / Craig Fraser**

The original character of this venerable villa determined the nature of its interior design. Each room is dominated by classic antiques from the colonial era, artfully mixed with tribal, ethnic, and religious objects. The juxtaposition of old and new ironwork is striking.

Die originelle Bauweise dieser alten Villa bestimmte auch die Innengestaltung. Alle Räume werden von klassischen Antiquitäten aus der Kolonialzeit beherrscht, die sich mit religiösen und ethnischen Kunstwerken sowie Stammeskunst mischen. Besonders erwähnenswert sind die alten und auch die zeitgenössischen Schmiedeeisenarbeiten.

La personnalité originale de cette ancienne villa fut un facteur déterminant du design intérieur. Dans chaque pièce prédominent les antiquités classiques, propres de l'époque coloniale, mêlées aux objets tribaux, ethniques et religieux. Il faut souligner le travail du fer forgé des éléments anciens et contemporains.

El carácter original de esta antigua villa marcó un factor determinante en su diseño interior. En cada estancia predominan las antigüedades clásicas, propias de la época colonial, que se mezclan con objetos tribales, étnicos y religiosos. Cabe destacar el trabajo en forja de hierro tanto de elementos antiguos como contemporáneos.

House in Alexandria

Architect: **Shahira Mehrez**

Location: **Alexandria, Egypt**

Photos: © **Ricardo Labougle, Hugo Curletto**

This older home near Alexandria is a perfect blending of its historic architecture and the personality of the owner, who took personal charge of the interior décor. The cubic architectural shapes are complemented by European furnishings, African tribal tables, and Bedouin textiles. A true melting pot of cultures.

In diesem Haus in der Nähe von Alexandria vereint sich die alte Bauweise mit dem Charakter der Besitzerin, die es neu dekoriert hat. Die kubischen architektonischen Formen werden mit europäischen Möbeln, Tischen der afrikanischen Stammeskunst und Stoffen der Beduinen kombiniert. Hier findet eine wahre Kulturvermischung statt.

L'esprit de la maison, proche d'Alexandrie, réunit l'histoire de cette ancienne construction et la personnalité de sa propriétaire, chargée de la décoration. Meubles européens, tables tribales africaines et toiles bédouines tissées complètent les formes architecturales cubiques. Un véritable métissage de cultures.

El espíritu de la casa, situada cerca de Alejandría, reúne la historia de esta antigua construcción y el carácter de su propietaria quien se ha encargado de la decoración. Las formas arquitectónicas cúbicas se complementan con muebles europeos, mesas tribales africanas y telas tejidas por beduinos. Un verdadero mestizaje de culturas.

Lake Manyara

Architect: **Chris Browne**

Location: **Lake Manyara, Tanzania**

Photos: © **CCAfrica**

This refuge, built of local wood and palm fronds, is situated in the heart of a mahogany forest. Vast windows enhance the view of the lush vegetation outside. The interior is decorated with contemporary, understated pieces set off by local knickknacks and handcrafted furniture.

Diese Hütte aus dem Holz der Region und Palmwedeln befindet sich im Herzen eines Mahagoniwaldes. Aus den großen Fenstern blickt man von drinnen auf den üppigen Wald. Die Einrichtung ist zeitgenössisch und diskret und wird von Schmuckelementen und handwerklich gefertigten Möbeln der Region noch unterstrichen.

Ce refuge, en bois local et en frondes de palmes, se trouve au cœur d'un bois d'acajous. Les vastes verrières permettent de profiter de la forêt luxuriante depuis l'intérieur de la maison, où un mobilier contemporain et discret est mis en valeur par des ornements et des meubles artisanaux de la région.

Este refugio construido con madera local y frondas de palma está situado en el corazón de un bosque de caobas. Las amplias ventanas permiten disfrutar de la exuberancia del bosque desde el interior de la casa, en la que un inmobiliario contemporáneo y discreto queda realzado por ornamentos y muebles artesanales de la región.

Riad and Minimalism

Architect: **Hugo Curletto**
Location: **Marrakesh, Morocco**
Photos: © **Ricardo Labougle**

The complex design of the original floors of hydraulic tile and the decorative borders, preserved and restored by Moroccan artisans, led to the choice of a minimalist décor. The charm of the district in which this home is located crosses the high, thick walls, adding a subtle atmosphere to the mix.

Die komplizierten Mosaikmuster der Originalfußböden aus Zementfliesen und die Sockel, von marokkanischen Handwerkern restauriert, bestimmten den minimalistischen Stil der Räume. Der Charme des bezaubernden Viertels, in dem sich das Haus befindet, scheint durch die dicken, hohen Mauern zu dringen und sich im Inneren zu verbreiten.

La complexité picturale des sols d'origine en céramique hydraulique et des plinthes, préservés et restaurés par des artisans marocains, ont déterminé le choix d'un certain minimalisme pour la décoration des lieux. La magie du quartier accueillant la maison traverse les murs élevés et épais parfumant subtilement l'espace.

La complejidad del diseño de los suelos originales de baldosa hidráulica y los zócalos, preservados y restaurados por artesanos marroquíes, determinó la elección de cierto carácter minimalista al decorar la casa. El hechizo del barrio en que se sitúa atraviesa las altas y gruesas paredes aromatizando sutilmente el espacio.

Earth and Wind

Architect: **Charles Boccara**
Location: **Ouled Ben Rahmoune, Morocco**
Photos: © **Pere Planells**

The restoration of this country house on the outskirts of Marrakech preserved the original character, not just of the architecture, but of the decorative elements typical of these buildings. The austerity of the color, from natural pigments, and the use of minimal furnishings are noteworthy.

Bei der Restaurierung dieses Landhauses in der Nähe von Marrakesch wurde der Originalstil so weit wie möglich beibehalten, nicht nur in der Architektur, sondern auch in den typischen Dekorationselementen. Auffallend sind die Schlichtheit der Farben, die mit natürlichen Pigmenten angerührt wurden, und die sparsame Möblierung.

Cette maison de campagne proche de Marrakech fut restaurée en tentant de préserver au maximum son caractère original, non seulement à partir de son architecture mais aussi à l'aide d'éléments décoratifs typiques de ces édifices. S'affirment une austérité des couleurs, produit de pigments naturels, et la rareté du mobilier.

Esta casa de campo en las cercanías de Marrakesh fue rehabilitada intentando rescatar al máximo su carácter original, no solo a partir de su arquitectura sino por medio de elementos decorativos típicos de estas construcciones. Destaca la austeridad del color, logrado a partir de pigmentos naturales, y el empleo de poco mobiliario.

Villa Toscana

Architect: **Beezy Bailey**
Location: **Cape Town, South Africa**
Photos: © **Reto Guntli / Zapaimages**

In 1952, Lady Bailey's dream came true when she built this Italian villa in South Africa. Like a complete work from the palette of prolific artist Beezy Bailey, each room has its own color with varying tones, contrasting with fanciful furnishings in a harmony with maximalist tendencies.

1952 verwirklichte Lady Bailey ihren Traum und baute eine italienische Villa mitten in Südafrika. Wie ein komplettes, aus der Palette des Künstlers Beezy Bailey stammendes Werk sind alle Räume in unterschiedlichen Farben mit verschiedenen Nuancen gehalten, unterstrichen durch märchenhafte Möbel und mit Tendenz zum Maximalismus.

En 1952, Lady Bailey fit d'un rêve une réalité en édifiant cette villa italienne en Afrique du Sud. Œuvre complète jaillie de la palette du prolifique artiste Beezy Bailey, chaque pièce possède sa propre couleur aux tons distincts, le contraste étant assuré par un mobilier de légende, en une harmonie tendant au maximalisme.

En 1952 Lady Bailey hizo su sueño realidad construyendo esta villa italiana en pleno a Sudáfrica. Como una obra completa surgida de la paleta del prolífico artista Beezy Bailey, cada habitación posee su propio color con distintas tonalidades, y queda contrastada por un inmobiliario de fábula, en una armonía de tendencia maximalista.

Beach House

Architects: **Nicolette & Philip Tyers**
Location: **Port Elizabeth, South Africa**
Photos: © **Reto Guntli / Zapaimages**

Rustic elements, such as wooden beams, clay tile floors, and the exposed brick and stone that accent the walls, make this weekend home a warm and cozy place. Animal skin motifs enrich the furnishings and draperies with varied textures.

Die rustikalen Elemente wie die Holzbalken, der Boden aus Tonfliesen, unverputzte Ziegel und Steine an den Wänden machen das Wochenendhaus zu einem warmen und einladenden Ort. Die Motive aus Tierfellen bereichern mit ihren verschiedenen Texturen die Möbel und Gardinen.

Les éléments rustiques – poutres de bois, sol aux carreaux d'argile ou brique et pierre apparentes revêtant les murs – font de cette résidence de week-end un espace chaleureux et accueillant. Les motifs de peaux d'animaux enrichissent d'une variété de textures les surfaces des meubles et rideaux.

Los elementos rústicos, como las vigas de madera, el suelo de baldosas de barro o el ladrillo y la piedra a la vista que reviste las paredes, hacen de esta residencia de fin de semana un espacio cálido y acogedor. Los motivos de pieles de animales enriquecen con variadas texturas las superficies de muebles y cortinas.

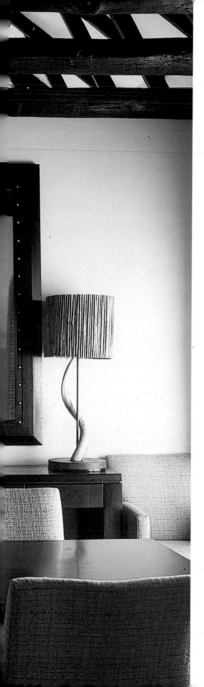

Dar Kawa

Architect: **Quentin Vilboux**
Location: **Marrakesh, Morocco**
Photos: © **Manolo Yllera**

Typically, riyads have austere facades which are closed to the exterior and are built around a courtyard with a central fountain. Dar Kawa has been restored to its original condition; even the original floor was refurbished with bricks made of clay in imitation of the traditional method.

Typisch für Riads ist die nüchterne, nach außen geschlossene Fassade und die Konstruktion um einen Innenhof mit einem Brunnen im Zentrum. Dar Kawa gewann durch eine sorgsame Restaurierung diesen ursprünglichen Charakter zurück. Sogar der Originalboden wurde mit Tonziegeln nach traditioneller Methode wiederhergestellt.

Les riads se caractérisent par une façade austère fermée sur l'extérieur et leur disposition autour d'un patio doté d'une fontaine en son centre. Dar Kawa recouvra sa personnalité grâce à la restauration menée à bien. Le sol d'origine fut même restitué avec ses briques d'argile fabriquées selon la méthode traditionnelle.

Los riads se caracterizan por su austera fachada cerrada al exterior y por estar construidos alrededor de un patio con una fuente en el centro. Dar Kawa recuperó su carácter original gracias a la restauración llevada a cabo; incluso el suelo original fue restituido con ladrillos de barro fabricados imitando el método tradicional.

287

Art and Seduction

Architect: **Chez Amidon**
Location: **Marrakesh, Morocco**
Photos: © **Pere Planells**

The heart of the carpeted courtyard is an enormous fountain boasting a beautiful example of Arab calligraphy, one of the most important pillars of Islamic art. Opposite, a seductive lounge, and its sofas with their soft cushions, invite the visitor to rest in comfort and enjoy the ritual of the traditional mint tea.

In dem mit Teppichen ausgelegten Hof befindet sich ein großer Brunnen, an dem ein schönes Beispiel arabischer Kalligraphie zu bewundern ist, einer der wichtigsten Pfeiler der islamischen Kunst. Gegenüber lädt ein verführerischer Raum mit Sofas voller gepolsterter Kissen zum Ausruhen und zu dem typischen Ritual des Minztees ein.

Le patio couvert de tapis s'organise autour d'une énorme fontaine arborant en son front un bel exemple de calligraphie arabe, l'un des piliers de l'art islamique. En face, les sofas aux multiples coussins d'une salle séduisante invitent au repos confortable afin de profiter du typique rituel du thé à la menthe.

El alfombrado patio tiene como núcleo una enorme fuente en cuya cabecera encontramos una bella muestra de caligrafía árabe, uno de los pilares más importantes del arte islámico. Enfrente, una seductora sala invita con sus sofás llenos de mullidos cojines a descansar cómodamente para disfrutar del ritual del típico té a la menta.

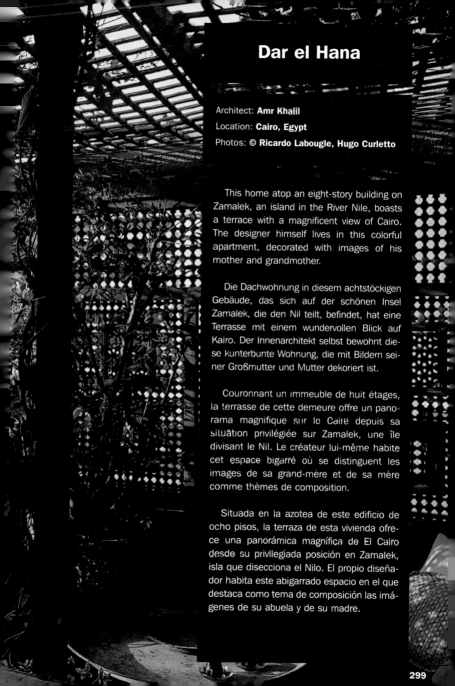

Dar el Hana

Architect: **Amr Khalil**
Location: **Cairo, Egypt**
Photos: © **Ricardo Labougle, Hugo Curletto**

This home atop an eight-story building on Zamalek, an island in the River Nile, boasts a terrace with a magnificent view of Cairo. The designer himself lives in this colorful apartment, decorated with images of his mother and grandmother.

Die Dachwohnung in diesem achtstöckigen Gebäude, das sich auf der schönen Insel Zamalek, die den Nil teilt, befindet, hat eine Terrasse mit einem wundervollen Blick auf Kairo. Der Innenarchitekt selbst bewohnt diese kunterbunte Wohnung, die mit Bildern seiner Großmutter und Mutter dekoriert ist.

Couronnant un immeuble de huit étages, la terrasse de cette demeure offre un panorama magnifique sur le Caire depuis sa situation privilégiée sur Zamalek, une île divisant le Nil. Le créateur lui-même habite cet espace bigarré où se distinguent les images de sa grand-mère et de sa mère comme thèmes de composition.

Situada en la azotea de este edificio de ocho pisos, la terraza de esta vivienda ofrece una panorámica magnífica de El Cairo desde su privilegiada posición en Zamalek, isla que disecciona el Nilo. El propio diseñador habita este abigarrado espacio en el que destaca como tema de composición las imágenes de su abuela y de su madre.

Tree Houses

Architects: **Van der Merwe Miszewski Architects**
Location: **Cape Town, South Africa**
Photos: © **Van der Merwe Miszewski Architects**

This private home adapts mimetically to its surroundings on Table Mountain, a mesa typical of Cape Town's landscape. This integration is made possible by its framework of branched posts, resembling artificial trees, the transparency of the walls, and the materials used.

Dieses eigenartige Wohnhaus passt sich an die Form des Table Mountain an, ein Hügel, der die typische Form einer Hochebene der Landschaft in dieser Stadt hat. Seine Struktur aus sich verzweigenden Säulen, die Bäumen ähneln, und die Transparenz der Mauern und des verwendeten Materials machen diese Integration möglich.

Cette demeure particulière s'adapte de façon mimétique au cadre de Table Mountain, une colline en forme de table caractéristique du paysage de cette ville. Sa structure de piliers ramifiés – des arbres artificiels – et la transparence des murs et des matériaux employés facilitent cette intégration.

Esta particular vivienda se adapta de forma mimética al entorno de la Table Mountain, colina con forma de mesa característica del paisaje de esta ciudad. Su estructura de pilares ramificados, como árboles artificiales, junto con la transparencia de los muros y los materiales utilizados, permiten esta integración.

Cliff House

Architects: **Van der Merwe Miszewski Architects**
Location: **Cape Town, South Africa**
Photos: **© Van der Merwe Miszewski Architects**

The location at the edge of a 45 degree slope and the spectacular panoramic view were the basic elements guiding the design of this house. Its rectangular proportions take on character thanks to the contrast of the two facades and the harmonic succession of decorative objects that enrich the interior.

Die Gestaltung dieses Hauses wurde durch seine Lage an einem Hang mit einer Neigung von 45 Grad und die wundervolle Aussicht bestimmt. Seine rechteckigen Proportionen verdanken ihren Charakter dem Kontrast zwischen den beiden Fassaden und der harmonischen Aufeinanderfolge der reichen Elemente im Inneren.

Sa situation, au bord d'une pente à 45 degrés, et le panorama spectaculaire du site déterminent le design de la maison. Les proportions rectangulaires la formant puisent leur personnalité dans le contraste entre les façades et l'harmonieuse succession des divers éléments enrichissant son intérieur.

Su situación al borde de una pendiente de 45 grados y la espectacular panorámica del emplazamiento, determinaron el diseño de la casa. Las proporciones rectangulares que la conforman cobran carácter gracias al contraste entre ambas fachadas y a la armónica sucesión de varios elementos que enriquecen su interior.

Ngorongoro

Architects: **Silvio Rech and Lesley Castens**
Location: **Serengeti, Tanzania**
Photos: © **CCAfrica**

At the rim of the Ngorongoro volcanic crater, this refuge, inspired by the clay-and-wood Masai farmhouses, creates a spectacular effect. Stylized structures and local hand-crafted ornaments are combined with decorative elements from the first colonial period to produce a luxurious, timeless setting.

Am Vulkankrater von Ngorongoro befindet sich dieses spektakuläre Haus, inspiriert von den Höfen der Massai aus Ton und Holz. Die stilisierten Strukturen und handwerklichen Schmuckelemente der Region werden mit dekorativen Elementen von Beginn der Kolonialzeit kombiniert, so dass eine luxuriöse und zeitlose Atmosphäre entsteht.

Aux contreforts du cratère du volcan Ngorongoro, ce refuge inspiré des fermes massaïs d'argile et de bois offre un effet spectaculaire. Structures stylisées et ornements artisanaux de la région se mêlent aux éléments décoratifs de la première époque coloniale pour créer une atmosphère luxueuse et atemporelle.

A orillas del cráter volcánico de Ngorongoro, este refugio inspirado en las granjas masái hechas de barro y madera resulta de un efecto de gran espectacularidad. Estilizadas estructuras y adornos artesanales de la región se combinan con elementos decorativos de la primera época colonial, creando un ambiente lujoso y atemporal.

El Mezour Riyad

Architects: **Jerôme Vermelin,**
Michel Durand-Meyrier
Location: **Marrakesh, Morocco**
Photos: © **Pere Planells**

The ornamental richness of this classic Moroccan house is present in every corner. In contrast to the fine textures produced by the architecture itself, in the fretwork, railings, and moldings, the furnishings and décor are austere, but make a powerful statement.

Dieses typisch marokkanische Haus zeichnet sich durch den ornamentalen Reichtum seiner Architektur aus. Im Gegensatz zu den feinen Texturen der Architektur selbst in Form von durchbrochenem Mauerwerk, Balustraden oder Gesims sind die Möbel und die Dekoration nüchtern, aber ausdrucksvoll.

La richesse ornementale de cette typique demeure marocaine classique s'affiche dans le moindre recoin de son architecture. Contrastant avec les fines textures de cette même architecture – claires-voies, rampes ou moulures – s'imposent un mobilier et une décoration austère mais également affirmée.

La riqueza ornamental de esta típica casa clásica marroquí está presente en cada rincón de su arquitectura. En contraste a las finas texturas producidas por la propia arquitectura, en forma de calados, barandillas o molduras, se plantea un mobiliario y una decoración austera pero al mismo tiempo contundente.

Summer Residence

Architect: **Stefan Antoni**

Location: **Cape Town, South Africa**

Photos: © **Reto Guntli / Zapaimages**

The spacious, bright interiors of this building on the outskirts of Cape Town gave the designers the opportunity to create cozy nooks using sliding panels. Discreet, cubical austerity is the ideal backdrop for paintings, masks, and other examples of South African art, which subtly add character in this home.

In den weiten, hellen Innenräumen dieses Gebäudes am Stadtrand von Kapstadt kann man mit Schiebepaneelen einladende Winkel schaffen. Die diskrete, kubische Nüchternheit ist der ideale Hintergrund für Gemälde, Masken und andere südafrikanische Kunstwerke, die dieses Haus auf subtile Weise prägen.

Amples et lumineux, les espaces intérieurs de ce bâtiment proche de la Ville du Cap permettent de créer des recoins accueillants grâce à des panneaux coulissants. Une froideur discrète et cubique est le cadre idéal pour les peintures, masques et autres objets d'art sud-africains, offrant subtilement son caractère au lieu.

Los amplios y luminosos espacios interiores de este edificio en las afueras de Ciudad del Cabo permiten la creación de acogedores rincones por medio de paneles corredizos. Una discreta y cúbica frialdad es el fondo ideal para pinturas, máscaras y otras muestras del arte sudafricano, que sutilmente aportan carácter a esta vivienda.

A Farm in Africa

Architects: **Steven Harris, Lucien Rees-Roberts**
Location: **Cape Town, South Africa**
Photos: © **Reto Guntli / Zapaimages**

The H-shaped symmetry of this restored farmhouse is reminiscent of the construction of some Dutch houses and establishes the interior layout: a large central area leading to four equal-sized rooms. The terrace begins inside the house, creating the subtle transition between interior and exterior typical of warm climates.

Die H-förmige Symmetrie dieser modernisierten Farm erinnert an alte holländische Häuser und legt die Verteilung der Räume fest. Von einem großen zentralen Bereich aus erreicht man vier gleich große Zimmer. Die Terrasse beginnt im Haus mit einem fließenden Übergang von Innen nach Außen, wie dies für warme Klimazonen typisch ist.

La symétrie en H de cette ferme restaurée rappelle la construction de certaines maisons hollandaises et détermine sa distribution lorsque d'une zone centrale spacieuse émergent quatre pièces de dimensions égales. La terrasse naît dans la maison, soulignant la légère transition intérieur/extérieur, typique des climats chauds.

La simetría en forma de H de esta granja rehabilitada recuerda a la construcción de algunas casas holandesas y determina su distribución de donde una espaciosa zona central surgen cuatro estancias de igual tamaño. La terraza comienza dentro de la casa, evidenciando la leve transición entre interior y exterior típica de climas cálidos.

Out of Africa

Architect: **Chris Browne**
Location: **Kichwa Tembo, Masai Mara, Kenya**
Photos: © **CCAfrica**

The tent-like fabric roofs evoke images of the classic Kenyan safaris of the 1920s and 30s. In contrast to this simplicity, the polished wood floors, solid stone walls, and luxurious furnishings in each of the spacious rooms add warmth and comfort.

Das von Zelten inspirierte Dach aus Textil beschwört die Atmosphäre der klassischen Keniasafaris der 1920er und 19 30er Jahre herauf. Die polierten Holzfußböden und die soliden Steinwände bilden zusammen mit den luxuriösen Möbeln in großen Räumen einen Kontrast zu der Decke, so dass das Gesamtbild sehr komfortabel wirkt.

Les toits de toile, en manière de tente, évoquent les scènes des safaris classiques du Kenya des années 1920 et 1930. Contrastant avec cette simplicité, s'imposent des parquets au bois lisse et des murs de pierre solides ainsi qu'un luxueux mobilier dans chacune des vastes pièces, offrant son confort à l'ensemble.

Los techos de tela, a manera de tienda de campaña, evocan el escenario de los clásicos safaris de Kenia de las décadas de 1920 y 1930. En contraste con esta simplicidad aparecen los suelos de madera pulida y las sólidas paredes de piedra junto al lujoso mobiliario de cada una de las amplias estancias, que otorgan confort al conjunto.

Classic Touch

Architect: **Pier Rabe**

Location: **Cape Town, South Africa**

Photos: © **Reto Guntli / Zapaimages**

The interior design project for this modern home in Cape Town, dominated by bright spaces and orthogonal shapes, incorporates classic details and gives the space a character all its own. A state-of-the-art kitchen is combined with an old-fashioned, rustic dining room and contemporary furnishings.

Ein modernes Wohnhaus in Kapstadt, in dem klare Räume und rechtwinklige Formen vorherrschen, die den Rahmen der Innengestaltung mit klassischen Elementen bilden und dem Haus seinen eigenen Charakter verleihen. Die moderne Küche wird mit einem rustikalen, traditionellen Esszimmer und Elementen zeitgenössischen Designs kombiniert.

Une demeure moderne de la Ville du Cap, où prédominent espaces clairs et formes orthogonales, est le cadre d'un design intérieur intégrant des détails classiques et offrant sa personnalité à l'espace. Une cuisine high-tech se marie a une salle à manger rustique ancienne ou des pièces au design contemporain.

Una vivienda moderna de Ciudad del Cabo, en donde predominan los espacios claros y formas ortogonales, sirve de marco a un diseño interior que incorpora detalles clásicos y otorgan personalidad al espacio. Una cocina de última generación se mezcla con un comedor rústico antiguo o piezas de diseño contemporáneo.

Riad Mabrouka

Architect: **Christophe Simeon**

Location: **Marrakesh, Morocco**

Photos: © **Pere Planells**

This riyad is another example of the architectural representation of the brightness, silence, and spaciousness that characterize Arab culture. Some rooms have vaults with delicate mosaics, while others have high ceilings and straight, simple lines.

Dieser Riad ist ein anderes Beispiel für die Umsetzung der architektonischen Werte der Helligkeit, Ruhe und weiten Räume, die für die arabische Kultur so typisch sind. In einigen Räumen gibt es Gewölbe mit wundervoller Mosaikdekoration, andere wiederum zeichnen sich durch hohe Decken und gerade, schlichte Linien aus.

Ce riad est un autre exemple de matérialisation architecturale des valeurs de luminosité, de silence et d'ampleur des espaces caractéristiques de la culture arabique. Certaines pièces présentent des voûtes délicatement décorées de mosaïques, d'autres se caractérisant par de hauts plafonds et des lignes droites et sobres.

Este riad es otro ejemplo de materialización arquitectónica de los valores de luminosidad, silencio y amplitud de espacios característicos de la cultura arábiga. Algunas estancias poseen bóvedas con una delicada decoración de mosaico, mientras que otras se caracterizan por altos techos y líneas rectas y sobrias.

Dar Tiour

Architect: **Bernard Sanz**
Location: **Marrakesh, Morocco**
Photos: © **Ricardo Labougle**

The arch leading to the courtyard crowns the entrance to this riyad, which belonged to surrealist poet Paul Éluard. Glazed ceramic tiles, furniture, fabrics, and rugs, intermingled with unusual collections, such as photographs of Muslim singers, create a baroque and kitsch arrangement, in keeping with the typical highly-ornate style of Moroccan décor.

Der Bogen zum Innenhof krönt den Eingang dieses Riad, der dem surrealistischen Dichter Paul Éluard gehörte. Kacheln, Möbel, Stoffe, Teppiche und kuriose Sammlungen wie z. B. Fotografien moslemischer Sänger bilden eine barocke, etwas kitschige Komposition, die gut zu dem typischen, überladenen marokkanischen Stil passt.

L'arche ouvrant sur le patio couronne l'entrée de ce riad appartenant au poète surréaliste Paul Éluard. Mosaïques, meubles, toiles et tapis, ainsi qu'une collection de curiosités comme des photographies de chanteurs musulmans, forment une composition baroque et un peu kitsch, au diapason d'une décoration marocaine chargée.

El arco que da paso al patio corona la entrada a este riad que perteneció al poeta surrealista Paul Éluard. Azulejos, muebles, telas y alfombras, junto con colecciones curiosas como la de fotografías de cantantes musulmanes, forman una composición barroca y algo kitsch, muy a tono con la típica decoración marroquí recargada.

THE GREAT
V.GRAMBY
MASTER OF MYSTERY WITH HIS
MUSICAL VARIETY COMPANY

Grumeti River Camp

Architect: **Sylvio Rech**

Location: **Grumeti, Tanzania**

Photos: © **Manolo Yllera**

This rustic building sits amid a spectacular landscape near the Serengeti National Park. Masterful use of basic materials and techniques created an inviting, highly aesthetic, functional setting.

Dieses ländliche Haus steht in der Nähe des Nationalparks Serengeti und is von einer beeindruckenden Landschaft umgeben. An diesem Wohnhaus wurden einfache Materialien und Techniken mit einer solchen Meisterschaft eingesetzt, dass ein sehr einladendes und außerordentlich ästhetisches und funktionelles Gesamtbild entstand.

Cette construction rustique est très proche du parc national du Serengeti et jouit d'un paysage environnant particulièrement spectaculaire. La demeure surprend par la maîtrise avec laquelle matériaux et techniques rudimentaires sont utilisés pour créer une ambiance accueillante au sens esthétique et fonctionnel profond.

Esta rústica construcción se encuentra muy cerca del Parque Nacional del Serengeti y disfruta de un paisaje circundante de gran espectacularidad. La vivienda sorprende por la maestría con la que materiales y técnicas rudimentarias se utilizaron para crear un ambiente muy acogedor y con gran sentido estético y funcional.